(Dis)placement

(Dis)placement
© 2020 Esteban Rodriguez

Published by Skull + Wind Press
Albuquerque, NM
skullandwindpress.org

ISBN: 978-1-7334253-2-2

Cover design by Adalis Martinez
Interior book design by Mark Cugini

Titles set in Kabel
Text set in Crimson

First edition, Fall 2020

(DIS)PLACEMENT

ESTEBAN RODRIGUEZ

☠ SKULL+WIND PRESS

PRELUDE

First, they will take your goats,
display their heads and flayed skin
on clotheslines, fence posts.

Village folk will gather. Speak
of He-whose-name-shall-not-be-spoken.
Speak of prophecy, holy books.

Your mother will cite chapter and verse.
And though you will mention
the boot tracks, note the discipline

of each step, the wind will steal
your words, and when the next animals
are killed—cattle burned, dogs

stuffed into plastic bags—you will watch
your village scramble, stack cinderblocks
and bricks into towers, section off

fields with barbed wire, simulate
escape routes, captures, and confer,
every evening by a fire, on what

they should do next: stay, fight, pack, flee,
or wait, like their ancestors had,
for God to riddle his wisdom in a dream.

BEDLAM

ASYLUM

They find me face up, skin like leather,
eye sockets flowered with maggots.

No shirt, trousers. Underwear torn
and soiled. And when you arrive to find

the crowd deciding how best to reuse
my socks and sandals, you contemplate

the last days of my body, imagine the rivers
I crossed, the brush I untangled, the terrain

rendered into our notions of purgatory.
You imagine my captors fit with berets,

bandanas, armed and camouflaged and ready
to place their prize in front of a camera,

or in front of their leader, who acting
as judge—the voice of and for the people—

lectures my body, it's broken sternum, ribs,
its bound and twisted limbs, its blood-

crusted lids flies will later lay their larvae in,
and from which they will hatch, bloom

from what darkness finds refuge in my skull.

LANDSCAPE WITH TREE AND LEG

Then you come across a tree,
and hanging from its branch you find

a leg—long, pale, severed cleanly
at the thigh. You walk beneath it,

study the chain bolted to its knee, study
the way the sun—searing the edges

off the leaves—cauterized its flesh.
And even though its nails are broken,

even though its soles are weathered,
redefined by days upon days of backcountry,

you make yourself believe the leg
is an installation, an avant-garde attempt

to say something about captivity,
war, or about the uses of the body, its ability

to evoke what you want from it
when you reach up, touch the ankles, calves,

feel the hairlessness in your palms,
and recall the weakness in your legs

when you saw your first death,
how your knees learned to kiss

the dark, unconsoling ground.

IN THE VILLAGE OF MISSING DAUGHTERS,

the sons, once a month, dress in their sisters'
garments, spend the night in skirts, blouses,

in frocks too small and tight for
their farm-worn and bricklaying bodies,

but perfect for the elders to reenact
their judgements, to question if such fabric

will be flaunted at brothels, or if the combination
of length and patterns is meant as courtship

for a husband, one who isn't thought
to be a cousin, or one who although might

have a limb missing, and whose fortune
dwells in a herd of goats and old recipes,

knows that when the moon sprawls into embers
across the fields, and the wolves cease

their soliloquies, night, that ancient accomplice,
will lead the thieves to another house,

and will watch as the daughters, leaning
from their curtained windows, are sung to,

serenaded, gifted a ballad of promises,
and lured—spellbound and half-clothed—

onto wagons, carts, or onto the backs of daughters
who've returned, and who laud to their supple hauls

of the love they'll receive in other worlds.

IN THE VILLAGE OF MISSING SONS,

the elders enter the cornfields at night,
clothe the naked scarecrows

in their grandsons' shirts, and with gas cans,
torches, with the ashes they sprinkle

as a final touch, set these ragged decoys
on fire, and watch, in a posture fit

for the jealousy of gods, as the symbol
they created melts, becomes charred wood

and straw, become masses the mothers
of the missing sons take down, haul home

through the morning fog, and place
at the kitchen table, where their boys stare—

if their buttons have stayed intact—
at the mush their mothers serve.

And while the mothers ask about their days,
and the sisters lick the chipped edges

of their plates, the fathers eat in silence,
unwilling to address an object their wives—

after supper—wrap in a blanket, carry back
to the fields, and nail to the crosses from where

they stood, and from where they wait—
as they gaze at the shriveled moon—

for what remains of their bodies
to be scorched anew.

AUGURY

Before the war, a child with two heads
will be born, and because the elders will deem it

prophecy, cast blame on our ancestors
and their sins, our mothers will corral their hens,

wring their necks, slit their throats, drain
their blood into saucers, bowls, then chant,

with their eyes gazing at the insides
of their skulls, prayers our lips have never known.

One by one, they'll visit the house, offer
blankets, cutlery, wooden dolls we carved

years ago, hoping our mothers would always
keep them, yet not surprised when they're gifted,

collected into an altar the two-headed child
won't see, just as he won't witness

the first wave of parachutists, or the tanks
set up as checkpoints, or the colonel

who arrives when the pillaging begins,
admires how far the fire's hunger extends.

SOMNOLENCE

But our prayers won't work.
And despite the cattle we sacrifice,

and the effigies we burn, God
will sleep through the first night

of fires, shots, through the morning raids
that will take our daughters, sons,

and that will keep the rest of us—
standing on the road with everything

we have—watching a colonel
turned judge lecture us, offer parables

we won't understand, then demand
we strip, bear the mockery of wind.

And when our nakedness fails
as punishment, he'll kick us

to the ground, and we'll be made to walk
on all fours, to howl like dogs

begging their owners to return.

LANDSCAPE WITH CROWD AND MAGGOTS

They will find you face down,
half-clothed, skin blistered

into hieroglyphs, limbs twisted
like roots unearthed. They will

hypothesize aggressors: wolves,
ghosts, shadows that feed on flesh

and bone. And as a man in the crowd
claims sorcery, explains the tricks

used on young girls, I will arrive
and contemplate your body,

the leaves in your hair, the scrawl
of dirt on your back, the maze

of maggots on your shoulder blades,
kissing the gashes the way

I'd kiss the space around your vertebrae,
believing my breath had the power

to heal, or to at least ease the pain
I knew you'd later feel:

the beatings, shots, the loneliness
when you watched the sun pierce

the sky, swell like a wound
bleeding out.

COOP

At night the guards gather,
chug jugs of whiskey, ale,

trade tales of love, conflict,
betrayal. And when their kill counts

become veiled claims for higher
rank, the drunkest one opens

our pen, picks his opponent out.
The rest of us turn, stare

at the emptiness in our hands,
and after bets are placed,

raised to see how long the bout
will last, we close our eyes,

listen as each strike redefines a chest,
nose, jaw, and till all we hear

are murmurs of prayers, blood,
of our names dripping

from a conquered mouth.

IN THE VILLAGE OF MISSING FATHERS,

the newest widows roam the fields
in wedding dresses, reciting the names

of all their children: Algol, Betelgeuse, Cetus...
And while their daughters lift the trains

scraping the soil, and the mothers name
a child with the next letter in the alphabet,

a son digs a hole behind his house,
tosses in his mother's ladles, brooches,

his sister's dolls, diamonds, drawing books
and dresses, arriving, hours later,

at his father's toolset: hammer, sickle,
a flask his father filled with ale

and ashes, and which he'd gulp
as he surveyed the fields, never once thinking—

if he thought anything at all—that his wife
would one day wander the stalks, chant

the names of apocryphal children,
and take off her dress when the moon

swelled to fabled proportions, casted
its glow on her frail and flimsy body,

and watched as she gave herself,
with the fervor she once showed her husband,

to the cold and fallow ground.

IN THE VILLAGE OF MISSING MOTHERS,

the strays that skulk the streets
are left unfed, and while sons spend

their days hand carving caskets,
and daughters make altars of their mothers'

earrings, necklaces, the men who still bear
the title of husband turn to poetry, utter,

shirtless and with the moon as witness,
portions of old epics, or portions of verse

they wrote on napkins, tissue, toilet paper,
on parchment they burned at the edges,

striving for authenticity, or for whatever noun
assumes they have the right to feel

the way they do, and that allows them
to scrawl metaphors they believe represent

their wives: a broken vase, a tire swing,
an empty house with the dinner table set,

or that desert they keep returning to,
tweaking the variations, but placing in each

a woman—chained by the ankles and wrists—
who watches the sun reclaim its throne, reign

over heaps of crosses and carcasses.

REQUIEM

And after your tribe rations the last
of its fowls, and the dogs you voted
to kill are skewered, stuffed quietly

into everyone's mouth, you let delirium
reign, see shapes that resemble food
in every rock, slope, mountain range,

in the mirages that scuttle the desert floor,
in the shadows that pool into more shadows
when dusk prologues a fingernail moon.

Your stomach begins to eat itself,
and as families break apart, as elders—
ready to become powdered architecture

for the ground—urge their progeny on,
you too find a place to rest, and dream
of a dining hall, a feast, of a table filled

with guests, none of whom you know,
and none of whom you're meant to know
when you see God seated at the end,

dressed not in the suit you expect,
but a uniform adorned with ribbons,
epaulettes, and with medals for all

the earthly battles fought, for all the lives
he allowed himself to spare.

MATRIMONY

No church. No priest. No father
to walk you down the aisle, no aisle

but the path you dream inside a cemetery,
worn with toppled gravestones,

ashen effigies. Barefoot, you walk
through it, avoid the shattered coffins

the way one avoids an ambush,
the way a body suspects gunfire,

bomb blasts, shrapnel. Beyond the hills,
firefights rage, and even as smoke

suffocates the sunset, and villagers
begin their exodus, you accept

you're wearing a wedding dress,
that your groom somewhere awaits,

and that once you reach him, trade vows
like secret documents, the soldiers

at the gate will neglect their duty,
and with the grace of rice throwers,

shower your exit with grenade pins
and shell casings.

THRENODY

Instead of music, your mother will shake
a jar of baby teeth, recite the names of moons
and constellations. Instead of a coffin,

we'll place your ashes in a shoebox,
place the shoebox in a trunk, and one by one—
father, sister, brother, friend—we'll take turns

dragging you from house to house, accepting
what gifts the elders give: sacks of wet rice,
loaves of soggy bread—all of which we'll smash

and leave as crumbs for the crows that trail us
up a hill, where the wind, a veteran to such events,
will deliver its eulogy, or what eulogy we'll hear

from its stammer, howls, from the sound of an ocean
that clung to it, and that grows when we close
our eyes, imagine waves frothing the shore,

returning, years after the war, the bodies of men
that never made it home.

ELEGY FOR A POSTWAR MOON

At your fullest, the elders set up court
outside the village, and when they finish

sharing anecdotes, parables, finish drinking ale
as part of their opening statements, they call you

as witness, ask to what extent you remember
the flyers, pamphlets, the rations that were dropped

with photos and bold-printed promises,
or the night the army entered with gas cans

and torches, baptized the barns and houses,
and quickly, methodically, bound as many sons

as they could capture. An elder speaks of sin.
Another of faith, prophecy. And because

they've each summoned God through doubt
and drunken prayers, and have yet to hear

his testimony, they debate complicity,
and all night, as the stars assume the role of jurors,

ask why you stood by, watched the beatings,
executions, listened to the soldiers demand allegiance,

or to the cries of the grandmothers who now,
as dawn froths the horizon, wade into the fields

with pots and pans, shoo away the crows perched
on their sleeping husbands, expecting that once they haul

their better halves home, they'll return to find you
still cuffed to the darkness, shaken, exhausted,

and ready to admit to any version of their story.

COLCHIS

All night, the ocean burns,
and when dawn rises without

an alibi, blurs the epilogue
of flames, a set of failed argonauts—

chained together at the hip—
begin cleansing the shore,

trudging through pools of oil,
through whale and seal carcasses,

through plane wreckage spread evenly
along the sand. Piece by piece,

the men haul their shares: glass, metal,
the mangled edges of a wing.

And when they've stripped the circuitry
from the cockpits, deveined the insides

of an engine, they reenter the ruins,
fill their wagons and wheelbarrows

with asterisks of bone, with limbs
that have been twisted into crude

punctuations, or with flesh that's become
a language these men no longer speak,

but which they remember,
and which they mutter as softly

as you mutter your name beneath
the rubble, hoping your voice,

rising like embers, won't be cauterized
by the eulogy of wind.

THEOPHANY

Doused in a froth of dawn,
your god appears before you,
and you take his hand, lead the boy

he assumed the shape of
through labyrinthine mirages,
through miles of sagebrush,

emptied suitcases, skulls wrapped
in plastic bags. And when—days later—
the heat settles, renders a desert

into focus, you drag your god
beneath the swollen shadow of a cactus,
tie his hands behind his back,

fill his mouth with dirt and branches,
and stagger—as you confess
your oldest sins—toward evening's

best attempt at closure, knowing
that if impulses had played out,
you would have cradled the shriveled

figure your god had become, laid him
by a bush, and—while chanting fragments
of a prayer—smashed his head with a rock,

and watched as darkness curdled out,
formed a puddle whose reflection
didn't show your face staring back.

EXODUS

PSALM

Praise be

   the days we wait,
the nights we sleep, the twin beds,

ceiling fan, TV. Praise the hour
the signal comes, the urgency

to grab our backpacks, leave.
Praise the town, the streets.

Praise the moon—full and on patrol—
as it looks away, lets us reach the edge

of town unseen, where, after bags
are checked, and names assigned,

I see myself not as me, but as a body
I slip into when the group begins

to move, when a greater darkness
anoints the path I gift my feet.

TERRA

DIASPORA

I.

First, an exodus of sweat, trails of salted rivulets
crowned like crucifixion thorns to your head.
Each bead, larger with every breath, surrenders
to gravity's custody, then migrates down your temples
till it reaches the unshaven borders of your jaw.
As the heat calcifies your already calcified skin,
and the shirt your country exports remains pasted
to your back, the perspiration drips onto the backside
of your backpack-clenched hands, and kisses
the shadow of your feet, while the ground,
still committed to its drought, clumps like soil
once acquainted with the affection of rain.

II.

Head hung, heavy, mute, you tread the barbed terrain
without your shadow, watch the castrated ground
fossilize your tracks. Despite the measured length
between each step, the horizon makes no distinction
between what moves and doesn't, and the mirages,
yawning across the plains, gnaw the floating cities equally
from everyone's view. Behind you: thin and shadow-
thirsty bodies with teenage faces; middle-aged and ash-
complexioned men who—as they fall behind and attempt
to remember their forged backstories and names—
imagine factories where their hands will learn a language
of meat and poultry, where this desert will bleed
into a desert of parking lots, and where they'll wait
all afternoon for pickup trucks, posture themselves
in ways that will get them chosen.

III.

Then decomposition. The moment
when the sagebrush just above your body
casts its shadow, and the shadow burrows
through your clumps of branded fabric,
through your flattened limbs drained
of muscles, cartilage. Day and night
carry out their cycles, render everything
stagnant. The scene begs for a wake
of buzzards, for their clichéd hovering,
their descent on the blackened bones
and bile, and their methodic picking
of the heart in its ultimate metaphorical
condition. But not every death translates
into a preconceived notion of what death is,
and instead, your body merely lies there,
secreting its tissue back inside itself;
no passing tumbleweeds to offer this image
a sense of closure, or to add a symbolic
element beyond the elements of exposure—
how your flesh coagulates into an object
patrolmen stumble on, photograph, haul out
and leave, with a numbered tag hanging
from your toes, on a cold, steel table.

IV.

Above the endless stretch
of stenciled vegetation, dusk
blots the sky to the mood
of cigarette ash. The sun
dissolves. Darkness weaves
between a group of men and women,
who focus, with every step,
on bearing the sharp and incoherent
spurts of winds, and on ignoring
the thought that when nightfall
tosses its body bag across
the swollen plains, the wolves
will come out and haul
the newest bodies away.

V.

And yet, the leader rises,
rubs anything off his skin
that might link him as night's
accomplice, aware that soon
his group will cross another day's
worth of mirages, and that one, two,
perhaps a handful of clients
will fall behind, be abandoned.
He surveys the sleeping bodies—
their limbs aligned into question marks,
their heads resting between piles
of backpacks, trash, blankets—
then moves slowly past them,
and watches the sun chalice into
a panorama, its glow bruising
the jagged horizon, like an old wound
refusing to heal.

VI.

Before us lie duffel bags, backpacks,
salt-encrusted shirts, torn and dusty pants,
forged birth certificates, deodorant, toothpaste,
tampons, notebooks, wallets, pill packets,
canned meat, chocolate bars, crackers, hair gel,
foot powder, duct tape, Band-Aids, gauze,
muscle cream, mirrors, rosaries, candles, crucifixes,
cut and modified milk jugs, water bottles covered
in plastic bags, boots and sneakers worn beyond
repair, cowboy hats, baseball caps, knots
of tangled hair, and bundles of faded photographs
that along with the rest of this inventory,
will receive a short description, be cataloged
for hours in small, air-conditioned rooms.

VII.

For the woman who can't keep up,
who from the back watches you
and the men take another step,
she must exchange another stretch
of passage for her blistered limbs,
for a few stifled minutes with the leader—
her breath and breasts heavy
with his sweaty silhouette,
and with the knowledge
that when he's done, her body
might be used again, emptied
of everything it has to offer,
and dragged to the middle of the desert,
where she'll lie staring at the tree
above her, gazing at the way
her underwear sways
like an ornament.

VIII.

As dawn unscales the last scabs of darkness, miles
upon half-lucid miles of saguaro appear before you,
each with a handful of severed doll heads hanging
from their arms. You move through this forest, study
their faces, the porcelain chipped, cracked, and faded,
deprived of the manufactured-painted lips that once
made it easy to mouth speeches to their jaws. You look down,
notice pieces of your unemployed flesh slipping along
your bones, and when chunks of your thighs and calves
reach the ground, scuttle and hide in the nearest hole,
you begin scooping the scalped and earless skulls,
the tiny suits and dresses, the shoes that drift like flower
petals from your hands, as you descend into a valley
of powdered carcasses, knotted hides, horns and pelvises,
and spinal columns the earth, for reasons you'll never know,
has kept perfectly intact.

IX.

From the far corner of your country, you survey
the expired soil, the heat-warped, corrugated
sheet metal meant to resemble the walls of houses,
the planks of uneven wood acting as rooftops,
the flaccid clotheslines strung between them,
and the half-clothed children stepping through puddles
haloed with newborn mosquitoes. Along the foot-worn
paths, you spot groups of seated women—bandaged
in handmade serapes—waiting for something
they were certain some god had promised. The ocean
smuggles in a band of swollen clouds, and you,
like an amateur prophet, know the coming forecast
will only tease the harvest, that the sun will again
bruise another season, and you'll be left walking back
to your village, picturing the frayed and nameless figure
your body will soon become.

LIMBUS

GENESIS

Doused in a froth of dusk,
you rise like an old god,

half-clothed, alone, made of flesh
the desert has gouged, gashed, torn,

severed in more words than you have
the language for, but which you want,

eager to ascribe myth to your battered bones,
or to convey, through fable and faith,

why you stalk the valley as a mass
of tattered skin, as a figure whose feet

must solve the maze of shattered ribs,
and who, days later, when ashes speckle

the ground, begins breaking apart spines
and skulls, and with their chunks and shards

builds pyramids, shrines, obelisks
you dedicate to yourself, so that like a god

your reign one day can be denounced,
and you can watch your kingdom fall,

burn before you're casted out.

HOSTAGE

You awake to a body not your own,
and with it fall in line, follow capped

and faceless men up a hill, a bluff,
a mountainside, up inclines with more names

than you own, and which you give
your new limbs to when daylight kneels,

pledges itself to night's airless throne.
Moonlight reigns. Creatures howl.

And between the shrieks and grunts,
between intermissions of teeth splitting

bone, you picture yourself before this self:
young, alone, crossing fields filled

with heaps of metal, plastic, clothes,
with mounds of trash you dig through,

unsure what you're looking for, but certain
of how sharp it should feel, and of how,

when the time comes, you will place it
on your throat, gaze at the sky, and offer,

without speaking a word, this body
for something greater in return.

REVERIE

That winter, at the top of a hill
you spent each night climbing,
you'd stop to watch the constellation

of cities below burning; the drowsy
architecture desecrated by a myriad
of armies: brick walls torched, streets

marauded, bodies piled onto carts
and dumped throughout the ash-coated
alleys, as though the soldiers that carried

them were fulfilling a laundry list
of prophesies, willing themselves
within kissing distance of God's feet

and shadow. The screams were unending,
and though you were sure you heard
your name amongst the thousands

of names uttered each evening—
the syllables doused in lighter fluid
and gunfire—you'd shut your eyes

even tighter, wait till the kaleidoscope
of morning melted over the horizon,
illuminated the acropolis behind you,

where again you'd find mounds
of elephant carcasses, statues of naked
men with their kneecaps and hands

missing, tangled banners with faded

headshots and hieroglyphics, censored
leaflets splayed across the marble steps

you'd slowly ascend, each stride
a pilgrimage, each breath a ceremony,
the fragments of which you'd blow

onto the altar of your palms, and which
would give you the illusion of warmth
when you – expecting to see skeletons

of armor, spider webs stretched
from pillar to pillar, silhouetted limbs
sweeping across the crumbling parapets—

would walk inside and come upon
rows of TV sets glowing with news
anchors, pundits, children with rifles

and bandanas, missiles flaring
from some colonized ocean, nightly game
shows, soap operas, static, static.

The bowels of that citadel would digest you
slowly, lead you through hallways,
corridors, passages you'd tiptoe

and crawl through for hours before
you discovered a cage in the middle
of a skull-shaped room, where a goat

always stood, tethered to a small
pole, pacing calmly back and forth,
content as it chewed on a piece of plastic,

and as it gazed at the knife you found
yourself holding, at how you turned it
toward your torso, ready to guide

its fated trajectory.

INHERITANCE

And when the last one falls,
claim his hat, backpack, wallet.

Claim the holy book scorched
in his back pocket. Claim his blue jeans,

shirt, the boots he wore for days,
believing, even when his skin lost faith,

quickly rotted, that his trek would soon
end, and that where his face now melts

would become, as if by fate, a stretch
of highway, town, the edge of a parking lot

where he and other men could wait,
forget, as shadows of trucks serrate

the pavement, the weight his feet felt,
and how, when a man fell, heaved

expired prayers on the ground,
he'd stop and kneel, accept, like you

and all the rest, what the body
was compelled to pass down.

CUPIO DISSOLVI

After weeks of desert,
you stagger back, follow

the trail of things you dropped:
wallet, shirt, rosary, rags.

And though you collect them all,
vow to undo how fruitless

they've become, you forget
your oath when you find,

amongst mounds of crushed
water bottles and cans,

your shadow spilling from a torn
plastic bag. Shriveled, scorched,

it flinches at first touch, squirms
from jug to jug, burrows itself

beneath the sand, and when
you snatch it up, squeeze it

with what strength you still have,
it squeals, writhes, confetties

the ground as you smear it
on your arms, jam in your mouth,

and as you hoist what remains
in the air, wave a piece,

to no one but yourself,
like a tattered white flag.

NEPHILIM

At dawn you emerge,
and with the river still cleaved

to your skin, you spot them,
a group of angels, bloodied, confused,

sitting with their wings torn, broken,
bent, as if they'd been shoved

from heaven, sentenced to earth
as punishment. Broken haloes in hand,

they shake their heads, grunt, scream,
argue with each other like men.

And though a part of you believes
that's exactly what they are—

a party lost and searching for a way out—
you insist you see, even as you stagger

near, white tunics, armor, swords,
and a certain hope that although

they've fallen, been stripped of trust,
glory, miracles, the sky will soon clear,

and the light that breaks the clouds
will deem some sins forgivable.

REVERIE

While you walked the streets of a city
that couldn't wake from hibernation,
stopped at every store window

and attempted to place the melting pieces
of your face back together, I crossed
a desert border into another winter,

where the sun, unable to remain
a metaphor against curtains of fog
and darkness, poured the remnants

of its halo across miles of half-shrouded
saguaro; each story-high cactus standing
like an unemployed scarecrow, and each

adorned with a myriad of doll heads
pried forcefully from their sockets.
Some were eyeless, some had frayed

ribbons strapped to their mouths
or temples, while those closer
to what I thought was the center

of this forest were hanging from
their ponytails, swaying nervously
against each other; the craters

in their androgynous faces humming
like wind pipes, picking up momentum
the more I personified the breeze

that played them, and the higher
I ascended the pathways speckled
with old sets of footprints, listening

as the dolls strung a tune I knew
I should have remembered, but couldn't,
even as I staggered between the batches

of saguaro and collected them, even
as I pictured you—fatigued and shadowless—
rounding another street corner, unsure

what you should make of the city
when it took off its mask, laid bare
its empty buildings, its cathedrals

of scrap metal and trash, its highways
soldered with corroded barrels and cars,
and that same dawn I too witnessed

when the wounded glow revealed acres
of carcasses and carrion; how soothing
my feet felt against the flesh, how softly

the bones broke open, as though the marrow
had something to confess.

AUTOPSY

I.

Note the head, the neck,
the pale outline of a chain
and cross on his skin.

Note the twisted throat,
sunken chest, the inked names
and iconography eulogized

by generations of dust
and wind. Note the way you note
this, and note, as you eye

his shattered pelvis, legs,
that despite the rot and stench,
his body is no different than yours,

because when you're done here,
leave the morgue and cross
a desert of a parking lot,

you too will begin to suffer
such thirst.

II.

Then you wake up, unzip
the body bag and climb out.

And when you've wiped
the grime from your eyes,

accepted your missing tongue
and jaw, you explore your wounds,

pull lizard tails and snake fangs out,
brush off the colonies of maggots,

ants, until there's nothing left
but layers of crusted blood,

and the confusion you felt
when, beaten and gagged,

you were dragged across the desert,
dumped where you thought

your body would never be found.

III.

They found one in a milk crate,
skull nestled between his ribs, pelvis,

vertebrae. And this one they found
on the riverbank, bloated, bruised,

skin shriveled like rotted fruit.
A rancher found one at the edge

of his field, admired the lizard
keeping vigil on its brow.

And you remember how, as a boy
throwing rocks at a fence,

you found one near a bush,
certain the mound was a dead dog

or bag, until you approached,
cautious, slow, intent on prodding—

with a broken branch—the body's
gnawed and bitten flesh,

and the wounds that you, decades
from that moment, one night

wake up to, find on your arms,
thighs, ribs, and question not only

their origins, but how you got here,
why the room is dark, cold,

or why you've been cut open,
feel a hollowness in your chest.

PROCESSION

From the riverbank,
you see what the sun alleges:

shoeless men limping through
remnants of dust clouds, mirages.

One by one, they shed their blue jeans,
shirts, hats. And after some dissolve,

accept the ground as savior,
those who remain kneel together,

and without a word begin clawing
the earth, digging until—a horde

of skulls and shattered horns later—
they exhume a casket, reminding you

of the men you once buried,
or of the men you left in the dead

of night, and whose invented names
you say as these pallbearers

march toward you, sing, in a tune
you know you should remember,

the return of a son God left behind.

MATRIMONY

The river moans, and on the bank
we stand: stabbed, battered, bullet-riddled

and bruised, spit out by the river
with no place to go, and with nothing to do

but accept what the next scene gives:
a bride in a white dress, groom

in a black suit. And though they're faces
are burnt—blisters ready to burst, ooze—

we stare on, feel moved when they exchange
vows, or when they kiss, or when we begin

tossing rice on their heads, and watch
as they pace the bank, undress,

and without looking back dive in,
as sure as we were that when they emerge,

crawl toward a new land, they'll enter
the next phase of their lives cleansed.

REVERIE

Nestled in a nest of rustic constellations,
the moon flings its glow across the forest floor,
then waits for you to follow, to forget

why nothing has been placed into context,
why the pine trees keep on growing, swelling
to storybook proportions, why the owls,

perched in their regal postures, look
like styrofoam props strung to clothesline
wires, or why nightfall mimics the texture

of crinkled butcher paper, unevenly stretched
and torn. Nightfeeders skulk the maze
of branches, and as the wind gusts in

on cue, and the cardboard leaves rattle
their vague premonitions, you take the bait,
chase the moonlight as it plays hide-and-seek,

weaves between the folds of deciduous
darkness, until, like a small, disfigured creature
indentured to lead drifters to a destined point,

it suddenly sneaks away, leaving you to watch
your flesh, tender from the heat and humidness,
churn into wet clay, and drip so quickly

that you begin molding miniature versions
of yourself, hopeful that after you start a fire,
place the tiny yous in a circle, your doppelgangers

will come alive, prance back and forth and back
across the flames.

CONFESSION

Amongst the bottles, jugs,
the piles of melted t-shirts,

sneakers, socks, you find a skull,
warm, raw, ready to be cauterized

by the sun. You pick it up, shake
the darkness out, clear its cavities

of scales, egg shells, ashes.
And after staring into its sockets,

unable to deem anything else symbolic,
you feel the need to find its jaw,

to search the tatters of denim, polyester,
cotton, the mounds of tarp and plastic,

the backpacks and makeshift crosses,
until, amongst it all, you see it:

an arch of bone, fractured teeth,
and a snake where a tongue once rested,

hissing and ready to speak.

DISINHERITANCE

You bury the sunlight left
in your hands, then shut your eyes,

collapse, let nightfall calcify
the fetid holes in your skin,

let it shroud the remains
of your scorched and shriveled limbs,

so when you wake in the morning,
peel yourself from scraps

of gnawed hide, vertebrae, ribs,
you'll feel yourself as you again,

rested, intact, ready to trek
to the desert's edge, and ready,

if the moment comes, to sever
the shadow from your back,

splay it on a bed of rocks,
and after buzzards have had

their share, bless it for what creatures
will claim it for themselves.

REVERIE

Dusk completes its exodus
inside you, and you find yourself
in the middle of a pasture, your body

next to the body of a newborn calf
wrapped in its afterbirth. A breeze
kneels on its knotted hair. Flies

rise ember-like from the soil,
anoint their new king. You scoot
back, watch its question mark

of a spine slowly shrink, watch
its limbs deflate, as if the scene
were on time-lapse, and just

as the last wreath of daylight
sets across the earth, the calf dissolves
into papier-mâché, and you are standing

beneath the remnants of a piñata
again. A mother, father, sister and uncle,
foregrounded against figures dressed

in trench coats and gas masks, tilt
their heavy heads, shift their attention
from the wooden bat in your hands

to the null expression on your face,
then back to the bat and the black bile
on its tip. And after you stop staring,

wondering if mushroom clouds
will sprout behind them, wash everything
away, you grip the bat tighter,

look down and begin swinging—
over, over and over—at the intestines
of old newspaper, at the skeleton

of warped clothes hangers,
at the black and white crepe paper—
shriveled, useless, and frayed.

LIMBUS

The desert fades,
and you walk the field

it becomes, weave
through a maze of tractors,

barns, unraveled bales
of hay and straw, until,

days later, you reach
the edge – the sky pink,

the clouds singed,
the ground ripe

with the carcasses of goats,
pigs, with chickens nailed

to fence posts, coyote pelts
strung on barbed wire,

tree limbs, each a symbol
you can't decipher,

and each less important
than the scarecrow

in the middle, or than
the way you stumble

toward it, reach out,
touch its frayed

and mangled legs,
and like a convert

after crucifixion,
pray the kingdom

will soon be reclaimed.

ACKNOWLEDGMENTS

Many thanks to the editors of the following magazines and journals in which some of these poems first appeared:

Arts & Letters
Blackbox Manifold
Juked
Heavy Feather Review
Neon
minor literature[s]
phoebe
Puerto del Sol
Storm Cellar

I am incredibly thankful for the attention and passion Trevor Ketner has given this book, and for their commitment to bringing diverse voices to the forefront with Skull + Wind Press. Thank you to Tori Cárdenas and Cormac Fitzgerald for everything they do as well.

I would also like to thank Gabino Iglesias and Saúl Hernández for their literary insight, and for always willing to chat books, poetry, and everything in between.

Thank you to Adalis Martinez for such an amazing book cover and design.

I am forever indebted to Traci Brimhall and Cynthia Cruz for their gracious words. Your work inspires me every day.

Special thank you to Scott Schaedler for reading this manuscript when it was still in its infancy. Your encouragement kept me refining the book into the version it is today.

Lastly, thank you to Norma. I would not be here without you.

CPSIA information can be obtained
at www.ICGtesting.com
Printed in the USA
FSHW022210180720
71816FS